AF705799

Pain Of Creation

An Anthology

Seema Rathore

BookLeaf Publishing
India | USA | UK

Made with ❤ on the BookLeaf Publishing Platform
www.bookleafpub.in
www.bookleafpub.com

Dedication

Jai Ganesh!

for

MaaPa

Preface

Hidden Pandoras!

I have just written. There are neither explanations nor illustrations. It is exactly as my soul sighs, heart feels, and body senses. I write my hidden Pandoras. May be I fool myself, but that's the way It is. Those long conversations, long walks, bright and mild , and wild modulations of sounds , feelings , sighs, highs and , lows , images, emotions, sensualities purely mine. Those magical , mystical , mysterious spaces where the so-called stupidities, cravings , and yearnings originate. Where those holy sounds mount on me . Fingertips travel on hair loose ends of my mortal cage - caught in the eargasm that come from light years apart , giving me my existential blues.

Then , I am afraid of being unafraid of myself.

Acknowledgements

The time that has Passed !
And...
The time that Remains !

Those who all left !
And...
Those who all stayed !

1. The Pain of Creation

Thought!
You fascinate me -
Catch me if you can...
The illusion of imagination
In my mind - a mirage of creation
In the wink of an eye - just
a little time span.
A wet sensation , and now dry
A ramble In the park
A flower-cajoled butterfly.
Catch me if you can...
Now she flies high in the sky
The glimmer is vanished,just a little Spark
An artist's half completed Arch
Growing old , need 'memory plus'
Catch me if you can...
I am you child , I am your pulse,
Here it was, now it's gone!
Gone?

It's not a sketch undrawn,
Oh such a head ache...
Help me sweet muse,
My heart is at Stake!

2. Awakening

Awake my friend
Some one cares , Some one cares,
To the brim of the Heart
And you will know your part.
Tis going to be your fault,
Don't you try to break his heart.
Cries and Moans and Repentance
Will not mend the broken part.
Pride and Prejudices
Arrogance and Malices,
Shall often make you look smart,
But it all will soon lose the path.
Your Pride shall subside.

Hatred and Envy and Enemity
With handful of soldiers,
Shall ground me to humility!
Rise Shall I -
Fall eight ; Rise nine
Good souls walk beside

To save , to help , to guide.

(when I was in class 10)

3. What's in Date!

For all the joys that it brings,
For all the Happinesses -
A date is a date is still a date.
A deed of care reaching the right destination
At the most appropriate time.

A shower of soothing rain,
Humming in the ear
A cool gentle breeze ,
Reaching the brooding being
That waits
An ecstatic blooming spring.

The time is right
The thoughts are ripe
Fruit of sweetness to wish
A Happy Day.
For all the joy of refreshning resonance
In eternity sway.

4. Paradox Resolution

Paradox Resolution...

And she loved him all by her ears,
And not less by her eyes.
She couldn't know,
A little more closer was allowed -
a trembling thought , fearsome too.
A little more farther he had to go...
A sensation all shudders,
And she loved him all by her ears
And he still sang to her!

5. Poetica

All expressions of Passions
Reduce to numb impressions
Back to the Alphabets Order!

And Good Remain There...
Good to be.
Sans Taste
Sans Smell
Sans Salt
Sans Smile
Make it sudden.

Just a Prick,
Not more nor less -
Haven't the soul to abide by you anymore!

6. Fears

The March of Dawn ; The Battlefield.
Shakened ; Awakened.
I realise - I am forsaken.

O ' Shield ! Grace, where is my Shield?
Who's peeping and penetrating into the soul?
Tears ? Fears?

I shall one Day

Cast them away...
For one and for all...

(when I was in class 10th)

7. Roses underneath the Snow

Tiny tinted drops of reminiscences
On the ocean of mind-
Currents under and Waves above rising
Moments gone sweet and sour
By the journey in the painted vessel
Upon this tainted soul.

Memories in their rush hour,
Leaving scars on the floor.
While the soldier of life retired -
Caught as a prisoner of war.

The night seems long and Dark
Dawn isn't any far,

Arisen, Awakened.

A patient , faithful, hopeful cold hearth

Shall find
Roses underneath the snow.

8. One is not alone.

One is not alone
Life has immense gifts to give
I have no potential to receive.

The blue sky above me
The cattle on yellow fields
In the biss of company.

Why then?
Your heart is lone,
It's phantoms following along
To laugh and with you moan.

Life - makes me , shapes me not
I am the mould, I am the architect
The Road to destiny is not uphill,
I am in charge, to act upon the will.

Mind - fair enough to care about
Morning moorings of the Swallows

Symphonies in sight to overcome
All that is sorrow and despair.

(when I was in class 10th)

9. The Railway Platform

The platform!
It is always saying a good bye,
Meeting , Departing - repeating the same
Isn't the same side of the coin then?

A graffiti on the wall announces plain,
As the green flag horns aloud,
You got to depart
To meet again!

The joyous station - deserted
Now patiently waits for the next arrival
In routine .
Tea and parle G in the hand enthralled,
Charms unseen.

The joyous Station - Fears , waiting for the signal - now
'Soon arriving'
True!
Departing Sad ; Meeting Thrilling.

10. Be and It Is!

Realise!
Nothing is lacking
The whole world belongs to me!

I cannot be the Himalaya
Be a Pebble!
I cannot be the Oak
Be a Shrub!
I cannot be the Captain
Be a Soldier!
I cannot be the Expressway
Be a pathway leading to shrine !
I cannot be the Sun
Be a Star - shinning above !

Size does not count!
Victory is round the corner
For
Whatever you are
Wherever you are

Just Be and It Is...

Be good for Something
Be good for Someone.

11. The Morning Person

Sun hasn't arisen ; Moon still in slumber.
Stars all a dreaming...
Earth has opened her gleams
All new light in her eyes shine
Vitality subtly pushes the weariness backdrop -
Stage for a new day is all set!

Sunbeams on the window to devour
The laziness shunned,
Heart thumps; Mind meditates; Soul chants.
Body decked up for drills
Smiling at sunflowers,black-eyed Susan,
Marigolds and daffodils!

Sweet melody restarts, rhythm follows
At the music , all air throbs in activity.
Smell of the tea on stove winking at the marie in the
bowl.
Infectious yet intrigued news print,
Deluged with a plethora of thoughts.

Again the reminiscing heart
Upon my inward eye - struck
A blaze of long lost crony
Cannot stand, and can't even stop
On its way a happy pony..
Eyes ran barefoot - it responded too.
A walk to remember for minute or two...

The day is made!

Never shall I cease to be a Morning Person!

12. Only If You Love Me.

When the Sun Shine lingers dimly on the mountain,
Last lazy gleam hovering on western waters,
Birds in unison sing towards home after a day's Toil.
Then my thoughts shall come to you
As your eyelids droop,
Senses sleep.
Your heart's red oozing slowly pumps
Each drop to every vein.
You will then be in my company dear friend-
From when the farmers till the soil
Seeds digged into the deep.
Till the crops are ripened
Harvested too...
Ploughman all shall rejoice ; it ll be
Spring , and pongal and lohri Delight!
Yet...
You'll for a while miss me ..
And this will be will be
Only if you love me!

13. Nanu/Naani

(A Mother in the Making)
The good news has finally arrived!

Nannu Naani?
A voice tis pure , serene and defiant
Words are a cascade, soothing and silent.
Still unaware of the beauty - spreading pure innocence.
In the grim and gloomy world around...
It would match nature's sweet senses and sound.

Innocent God's angel with tender manners mild
Heaven's dearest lamb in joyous laughter wild.
Eyes - frothy stream flowing full of love
Face - sunny prism purest ray of Dove.

A heart so pure - so tender yet strong
Faith and trust within would never go wrong
Harmonious song in Cacophonous world
Jittery noise ; to a lullaby lulled.

A heart that yearned, a prayer went up
Heeeded - and hearth and home is beautiful again.
My heart does pine
So shall it remain.
My prayer I seal it with Amen!

14. The Transformulation

During my after dinner walks with you Didi,
My vulnerable watery being often surprised
By your words and laughter.
Laughter always left behind at the hostel
On walks not in your company...
' I choose Laughter' - you always said.

Not much time has passed
Since we departed for our respective stations.
A tearsome soul -
Tears rolling down the cheeks
At the slightest provocation!
Tears make you a Black Sheep
Laughter - You have so many friends
Tears - Your loneliness knows no end.

Time has slipped - keep inverting the sand clock
Time won't reverse...
Have the rivers of Tears dried ?
Laughter Have I then chosen you ?

Tears come, and they remain.
Still laughter comes and comes again.

Itinerary goes on to a destination unknown
Really to an extent , Have I grown?

15. DEATH rarely comes

I still remember the year
When two beautiful souls departed -
For Mother Teresa - Perhaps Time or THE CALL
For Lady Diana - I think didn't deserve such an end at
all!

Death rarely comes with an appointment,
Denuded forces of mind ,
End to all sentiment!

Men fight and yield not ,
It's the last moment
They know not!
RAM NAM SATYA HAI
in rythm rank and file
Ah! Life such a bubble
Terribly futile!

All that is Enterprise
All that is Hardwork.

All that is love and Care
And Smiles and Tears just not fair.
Giggles and laughs ; Swoon and Sigh
All freeze in words on the cold epitaph.

Some die old ; some die cold
Fate's cruel jaws swallow the young
Leaving behind the vacuum
For the laurels they had won.
Why Rush then
To carve that niche on the sands of time -
Dying to love
Dying to live !
An old traveller pointed to that grafitti on the wall.
" We shall pass this way Just Once"

16. Nanu.com.mom

A sharp mind for computers
Strong body for Karate
So! Nanu goes active...
Oh! Dear.
Tell me is it?
Computerised Karate?
Or
Karateised Computer?
Tuesday Karate,
Monday Computer,
You'll pass the Yellow Belt!
Just press
One key called Enter!

(The word Nanu comes from the Gujarati word Nanakdu, the sweet child in the cradle who keeps changing sides)

17. Roshu.com.mom

In the dark of the night
Rule fear and fright
Tunnel seems unending
Broken hearts awaiting mending
Did I see the horizon glimmering
Hot coffee , on it cocoa simmering
My own sky and it's golden sunshine
And Roshu only mine!

Roshu - Roshni [hindi- the Llight of life]

18. Fireu.com

No no! You are the hottest little thing in town tonight!
Your anger , your frown and my fright.
On a rainy day you are an umbrella
Blown away as the Kite.
passion so strong, so deep, so tender.
Heavens save me from your anger!
As creative as 'Java'
As hot and bright like lava
a Volcano in town -
Gone is the trauma
And in my arms remains
A passionate melting magma.

P.S - your anger comes ;your anger goes
Sweet love beneath ; forever flows.

19. Muse 2k

Deep!

Even the Hundred Thousand Songs
In my music corner,
Cannot Compare -
The depth of that one song...
Which you said - "I Like!"

Big Things Small !

When the task seems uphill
I have to wrestle with my will
Every one else seem a little busy
Special people come from beyond
To make things easy.

The good is Happening
The better is yet to come...
The best is following!

20. Because ! Love's in the Air.

I cannot wait anymore
To see you coming from Yore
Because! Love's in the Air.

Scorching Sun seems so much fun
Afternoon ride ; so smooth a stride
Because! Love's in the Air.

The Bridge, the rivulet, the isle,
The treehouse, the farmhouse,
The guava grove, field of sugarcane
Sweet and sour sing a new tune
In a new name -
Because! Love's in the Air.

The Journey uphill ; The Journey downhill
Spades and Hearts ; Passion and Thrill

Soft and tender snowfall
A morning slippery ice
Garlic slice - sprinkling spice
A Brewing...
Because! Love's in the Air.

A wonder or a divine thunder
No pain, no fear, no sorrow, no tear.
Because! Love's in the Air.

A Feeling full of joy is it?
Or Joy full of feeling?
Because! Love's in the Air.

Was it Written, was it Destined?
Or we a fortune Designed...
Because! Love's in the Air.

Cynthia so bright
In the Darkness of this night
All seems so right
Because! Love's in the Air.

Here is changed to there
Neither works , nor prompt nor part...
Beat misses the heart
Because! Love's in the Air.

Snail struggling
On a jet plane speeding
Because! Love's in the Air.

It's now 'where the wind blows'
It's now 'where the water flows'
Yet!
Life's stolen moments, beans spilt-
No fear, no pain, no guile, no guilt-
All is Joy
All is Fair!
Because! Love's in the Air.

21. In Pencil

How domineering! Reigning!
The tuneful moonlit, breezy calm cadence
As it pacifies my -
Absolute, Adamant, Egotistical Soul,
Illumined in the Afterglow
Of the chiming - beaconing Halo!

Why don't you be the symphony?
The rhythm that collects my crackling soul...
Why don't you be the verse?
That re-formulates the lexis of my being...
A captive - that i could reclaim!

Why don't you be the Author?
Who writes the script on his book -
Then -
Book would fall in love
again -

Soft music - Deja Vu.

22. The Dice

One - Take a walk down the street
Two - A fifteen minute walk
Three - Conscience knock knock!
Four - let's have some serious talk.
Five - Illusions , schizo lights glitter
Six - Alas! You're not immortal.. Creator's fragile Critter!

One - star sky-scraper studded city
Complexes, marts, clubs, discotheques
Two - a poliod child , the crooked leper
Curious at the traffic light chart of nifty
Three - street puppy hurt , a rushing car
Four - peeping pug at the windshield.
Five - striving...
Six - thriving...

One - its all in the mind
Two - nothing in my hand
Three - a king

Four - a caricature
Five - a Helmut Kohl
Six - RIP departed soul.

A Complicated tale-
One - a moment of success
Two - there you fail.
Three - love, honesty, success, power
Four - lust, corruption, tears, strife.
Quench not thirst of life...
Five - love in heart, living humble
Six - Politicians sorry, m out o' jumble.

23. Whirlwind

There is that brave little girl!
Always frittering at the curls...
Still untouched in any whirl.
A plane Jane...
Leaps and bounds at
Heart's quotidian aims..
Her colour is white, Her will Her might! She's not a
Peacock - Proud , egoistic, or selfish.
Life's beautiful ; a little
Devilish, urchinish, and elfish
Nature's wish Her friend, love her ideal
Blest! Softly slide in hours
Peaceful , harmonious, cordial.
Perhaps no Mission
Nothing to accomplish
Life a beautiful song
In time establish!
She'll go her way
In swing and sway...
Make her day

At any cost- follow her not
She herself is lost!
In passion a flower - her friend philosopher and guide
By the day slide..
Fall softly on earth by night. (some tender hand pick and drop in the soil)
Mountains She knows are forever there
Whispering winds hold her in care!
Nights were chilly ,
Heavens a pouring
Winds were thundering,
When she was born .
perhaps,
Blown away with a whirlwind
Then she'll be gone!

24. Poetica 2.

Words are asteroids in free space...

Mingling with the azure,
Flowing with the ocean,
Drowning in the vale,
Boomeranging , unbecoming,
Atomic roller coastering.

' What comes around
Goes around!'

' It takes two to a tango'
From whence they come
They Go...

[nothing Dies it only Transforms]

25. Rim!

How easy to move on and make new friends, How
difficult to treasure the old ones.
How easy to crave for new securities,
How difficult to realise the care that is.
How easy , the rave and rant for
New events,new circumstances,new fascinations,
How difficult to take stalk and organise
Past commitments,
Relations,
How easy - be material ; be practical
How difficult to understand the power of true love.
How easy to read Rumi,
How easy to read his ' Pir-O-Murshid'
Shams Tabrizi,
How difficult to drink' love - the water of life'

All that is pure
All that is genuine
All that is Wonder

How difficult to walk the fire- the soul of love.

kids in Iran , Syria and Ukraine yearn warmth and light
and Sunshine...
How easy to read - in - empathy - too far
How difficult to reach out and stop war.
Life - difficult and complex,
Ease - Attacts and Allures,
Dis-ease - Debarred and Demurred.

26. The Homecoming

Sunken Sullen Sun drowning in the vale of horizon...
A Qualis neatly sleeking the highway frozen
On the notes of -
' country roads take me home..'
Sweet and fair Diana smiling from the silver sky she
shone!
Soft Snowy fairy lights lighting up my world
Gate lamps and blushing shades lit up
Pets in their manger all lulled up -
' starry starry night on my walkman'
On the Ramble Road.
Next on the play list - ' take my breath away'
Superfast thundering on the Railway line
Steps swing and sway, my chilly spine
Soon Darkness dares me - my Shield invade,
Dawn is round the corner
Nightmares to fade!
Morning Rapture!
Please be on time
your tendril kiss - again

On brow of mine!

27. Don't forget to eat your Ice-cream

Action follows Expectation!
Expect not they say,
But players play
Never to lose ; never to last...
Paths of toil,days of glory
Dreams of beauty,brains of wisdom
Wars for power,quest for knowledge
Bustling bursting bubbles
Just a book or a short story!

Expect to live longer- watch 'Dr. Morepen'
Expect to binge - freak out at 'Macdonalds'
Expect to be Buddha - no more craving
Expect a safe life - savings bank account
Stay in your lane
A sage advice quite sane
' Eat half your hunger'
' Drink twenty five percent water'
' leave the rest for ventilation '

And Sensation -
Don't forget to eat your Ice-cream!

28. Strength

After a day's toil,
Couched inner turmoil.
Would my soul settle for less
But your togetherness.
Sweet are the senses of Departing,
They bear the fruits of
Meeting...
Difficuties i am facing,
To share unwilling.
Life isn't fair,
Not that easy - as I see
Not that hard - as I Understand.
I Bear with strength, strife and pain ;
Honour, that I might not stain!

love - the Centre
love - the Circumference
love - the Home

love - the fence

29. Until, the Silence is Broken.

Half a million children are dead - more!
Wailing mothers searching
Where have all of them fled?
Leaders and politicians
Hiding, burying faces
Indifferent, deaf and dumb
Humans stuck in rat-races.

Democracy undefended
Principles unprotected
Sovereignity strained...
motives,manipulations,maneouverings
Mean interests identified
United Nations in Limbo
Sheep in Kurds crucified.

Nations in nature and grandeur did smile
Gold in liquid, worth a while.
Prosperous,progressive, growing miles

Captive in vicious circle, sheep in exile.

What was their role?
Why were they born?
Darkness their fate?
Didn't they deserve their Dawn?
Cacophonous noise o human rights
Life denied, basic rights
Hounds and bulls tearing one another
In gory fight.

A creature in the desert, so ugly yet strong
Leukemia gripped..
A small price -
For all his wrongs.

30. Until, the Silence is Broken.2

The Buddings, The Ducklings, The Seedlings
In field ambulances throng,
In dispensaries - they don't belong.
They haven't begun to live,
Doom showing up !

Sheep chose not their shepherd -
So he did not care...
Muted remains poetic justice
Play - deeply cruel , unfair.

Sanctions, they say is the solution
Wars destroyed bodies, souls in demolition

Air, water, fruits, medicines, bread, wheat,
Rice - reservoirs are all empty
Who's paying the price?
Who's beating the retreat?

Lost are the lambs - fallen , forlorn, frozen
Sheep dying, how many will, for how long?
Until the Silence is broken!

31. The Flower Picker

She is Anon!
She is the Flower Picker.
Every morning she meets them
She waits for them to tenderly drop
Before that -
She let's them bloom
Spread smiles of joy
For one and all
As they wither and fall.
Her daily regimen,
Her daily reminder,
Mortal cage takes a bow,
A click, a pause amidst the flow-
A pilgrim's mental assurance
She picks them then -
The pink dahlia, the yellow lily,
The white belladonas
The periwinkles mostly...
Tenderly giving back to the soil
To soul. - back home.

Journey goes on..

Be Born,

Bloom, and

Back home.

32. There's a Flower Picker

One Day -
Perhaps it would be,
A warm Winter Morn!
On her morning Ramble
She shall stride on...
She will see
The Sun is one and weak
Clouds are too many
Playing hide and seek.

The blessed wrinkled - periwinkle
Tender and Soft as oft..
Shall quietly fall
And this time not rise...
A tender hand of some passer - by
Perhaps another flower picker
surmise.
Shall pick her , the blessed periwinkle
Pick her
Kiss her

Bid her a casual farewell
Put her back in soil , in the fence
And she'll be home
To eternal silence.

The cycle goes on... in the spiritual realm,
If there is one?
It'll be the night storm again
A bud in the dark bed -
Show up the shape of her heart,
Begin ,
With the same maxim -
' cleanliness is next to godliness'

33. If only I kept a little quiet

Sometimes in expensive luxuries of speech
I indulge, discordences screech and spill
Treasures of Silence are priceless still..

Pathless woods -
Save , lovely dark and deep.

Cold and dingy winds ,
Help me with your breathless words
As you cajole my cheeks and chin
Neither tongue nor lips remain
Unknown language you sew and spin.

Of words unspoken - who is the master
Of the spoken - all slave.

Luna roams the silent skies
Never for words does she crave

Petty matters, triping trifles, shallow notions
Seldom did speech such stormy oceans brave.

Waters are silent and they are deep
If only a little 'Quiet' I could keep.

34. You

Either take on life, You
Or let life take over You
Go, get what You want,
Or life will leave You with all You don't want
Go , grab what You Like
Or You'll have to like what You got...
Live the way, You want to
Or die the way the world wants to.
Make the choice You
Between good or bad
Or choose between bad and bad You.
Live with determination , You
Die in dignity You!
Or You go, mingle with living-dead
Because..
That's your destination!

Dont just keep saying in this mime
Please give me some time

And everything will be fine!
It'll be fine - yes?
Will it be fine - No?

35. Fireflies in her little shoe

As she walked, finding her way
Through the darkening woods,
A sparkle she saw
At the tip of her tiny shoes -
She had such small feet.
Suddenly she felt
A thorn-prick in her shoe
She bowed..
Pulling the pricking feet
Through the Black haze
She glanced At her shoe,
" oh how small it is- "
And " how big is my head"
Big head
Small shoe - too Small ,
For some one else to fit in.
The thorn was out , the prick was gone,
She had to walk on ...
Finding her way

Tearing through the spider mazes
She saw...
Some night lamps tingling in the distant plains.

36. What the Word.

Standing in the middle of the debris
of all my words -
Some kissing the mud
Some mucked - up
Some tainted
Some half broken urns
Some shattered pieces of glass -
In the same ,
I see my own reflection
I wonder
A Resurrection!
Better off -

If I owned a flour mill
Bid them all - those words
Collect them all - Herculean
Put them all in the mill
Ignition -
Grind them all ,
Then cook some bread

And at dusk...
Give them all to the hungry old women ,
Sitting on the sidewalks!

37. Niche

Dry leaves a rattling
Etched cracks a crackling,
Full fleet
Under my feet.
A sporty step enjoy -
Plodding plights deploy.

Life's momentous halted fleet,
Whose
Gifts neither perennial ,
Whose
Affections nor privileges.

From the deep deep blue -
A vampire's tinklings,
An urchin's inklings.
The Leo - bacchus' sprinklings,
Over life's amber'd pages !

Red wine, so old; so freshly soporific.

Silence, so brutish; so beatific.
Nestor's pantomime ; so loud singing
Parched, yet so brimming.

From the figment of imagination,
To niche in my heart.
It goes on churning
Till it ,
Sets the froth apart.

38. Oblivia

I do not know ,
What is that unbridled thought-
That holds the reins of my cerebelum.

I do not know ,
To what unknown incorrigible beat
My heart rythms incessently...
Forcing a nostalgia that lasts longer -
Than the thoughts of the moments gone by.

How de-populated the world around feels,
Longer Than the time that has passed away.

Reaching out then is all but a complusion
With under currents of futile repulsions

I know not when time will run out -
Dead again before death?
A heart vacated,
Mind accomodated of misnomers.

Time and Place I know not.
Strange fate,
Karmic circle...
With it I am fraught.

Deaf to all sounds
Blind to all geometry
Oblivious to all neutrons
How de - populated the world around feels.

39. Ram!

Ram is the Mahamantra that ShivParvati chant...
Ram is the adornment of Mahadev and Mahamaya...
Ram is the seed of Sun...
Ram is the seed of Fire...
Ram is the seed of Moon...
Light
Energy
Calm
Ram is Ved...
Ram is Purana...
Ram is Bhrama, Vishnu, Mahesh.
Ram is Aneeh, Anoop, Anama.
Ram is pure in straight...
Ram is pure in reverse...
Ram is Ganesha's favourite
Ram is the light revealed through Darkness
Ram is the water melting from the rocks
Ram Liberates
Ram is Liberation
What's in a Name?

Name is grace
Name is foundation
Name is solution
Name is Reverence
Name is Deliverance.
Name is Enough!

40. It Seems Like Yesterday - For MaaPa!

When my tooth decayed and fell ,
I realised how Paa ate his roti so slow and long.
When my eyes ached and blurred,
I realised Maa's spectacles needed to be fixed.
When I forgot my chores and I fumed in frustration,
When I started losing taking stock ,
When half the time of the day
Searching for my little nothings , I strayed
I cried - wished I had listened
When Papa always said ,
Beta make a list , keep a diary for each day.
Then I realised ,
How one Day he could not recognise a good neighbour,
He had only met yesterday,
Now When I am lonely
I realise how much MaaPa wanted
To talk to me and listen to me ,
For just a little while
And I in a pretence, ruthless, and vile

Replied I am busy -
Busy without work.
MaaPa have still kept their cheer
And I am alone in my fearful tear,
Because I know ,
Time like a river has just flown by -
Because I don't know ,
how much is left?
It just seems like yesterday, I sigh -
When Maa tied my hair and my laces,
And Papa took me by his hands,
To my First Day at School!

www.ingramcontent.com/pod-product-compliance
Lightning Source LLC
Chambersburg PA
CBHW070645240926
51846CB00003BA/788
9789375435990